HISPANIC LEADERS OF COURAGE

ROBERTO CLEMENTE

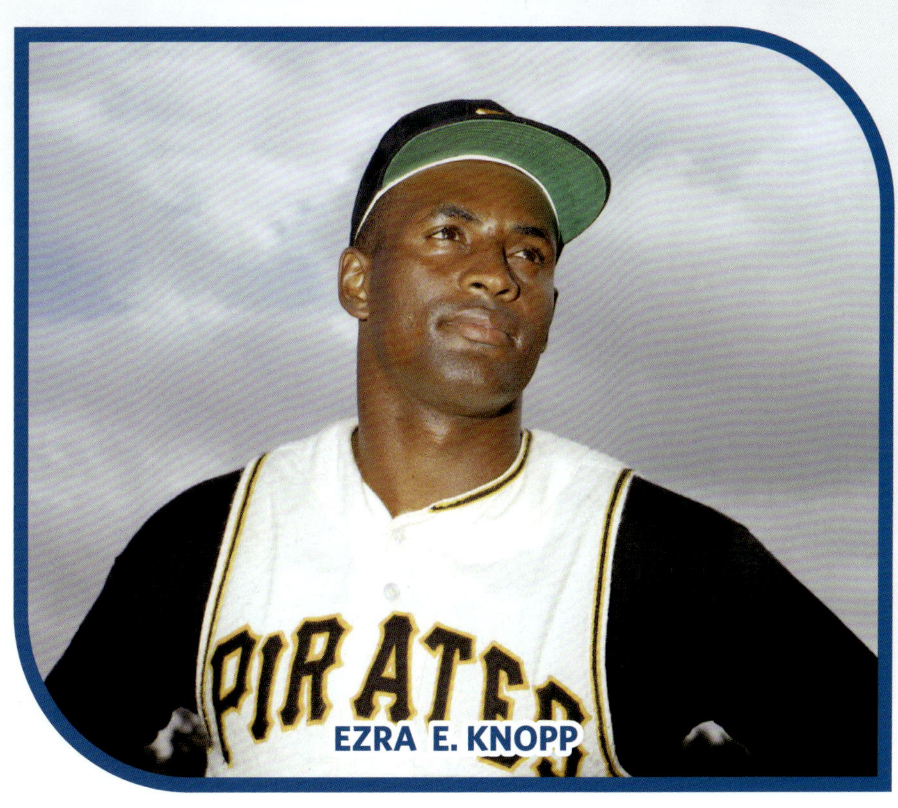

EZRA E. KNOPP

Published in 2026 by The Rosen Publishing Group, Inc.
2544 Clinton Street, Buffalo, NY 14224

First Edition

Editor: Nathalie Humphrey
Book Design: Michael Flynn

Photo Credits: Cover, p. 1 AP Photo; (series background) Sergei Mishchenko/Shutterstock.com; p. 5 IanDagnall Computing/Alamy Stock Photo; p. 7 Javier Cruz Acosta/Shutterstock.com; p. 9 JonathanCollins/Shutterstock.com; pp. 11, 13, 17 Globe Photos, Inc/Globe Photos/ZUMA Wire/Alamy Live News; p. 15 Alon Alexander/Alamy Stock Photo; p. 19 f11photo/Shutterstock.com; p. 21 Photo Win1/Shutterstock.com.

Library of Congress Cataloging-in-Publication Data

Names: Knopp, Ezra E. , author.
Title: Roberto Clemente / Ezra E Knopp.
Description: Buffalo, NY : Powerkids Press, [2026] | Series: Hispanic leaders of courage | Includes index.
Identifiers: LCCN 2024040120 | ISBN 9781499451139 (library binding) | ISBN 9781499451122 (paperback) | ISBN 9781499451146 (ebook)
Subjects: LCSH: Clemente, Roberto, 1934-1972–Juvenile literature. | Baseball Hall of Famers–Juvenile literature. | Baseball players–Puerto Rico–Biography–Juvenile literature. | Baseball players–United States–Biography–Juvenile literature. | Discrimination in sports–United States–Juvenile literature. | Philanthropists–United States–Biography–Juvenile literature. | Baseball–Social aspects–United States–Juvenile literature.
Classification: LCC GV865.C45 K56 2026 | DDC 796.357092 [B]–dc23/eng/20240913
LC record available at https://lccn.loc.gov/2024040120

Manufactured in China

CPSIA Compliance Information: Batch #QSPK26. For Further Information contact Rosen Publishing at 1-800-237-9932.

CONTENTS

Meet Roberto Clemente

Roberto Clemente was a baseball superstar! He played in 2,433 baseball games and had over 3,000 hits during his time playing. But being black and Puerto Rican, Clemente faced a lot of **discrimination**. Clemente fought for the rights of all people of color.

Carolina, Puerto Rico

Roberto Clemente was born on August 18, 1934, in Carolina, Puerto Rico. Clemente was a great baseball player from a young age. He learned to love baseball from his mother. When he wasn't playing baseball, he worked with his dad on a nearby sugar plantation, or farm.

Monte Irvin

Clemente went to a lot of baseball games in high school. At these games, he watched Monte Irvin play. Monte Irvin would later be part of the Baseball Hall of Fame, a museum that records the greatest baseball players. Irvin spent many winters in Puerto Rico.

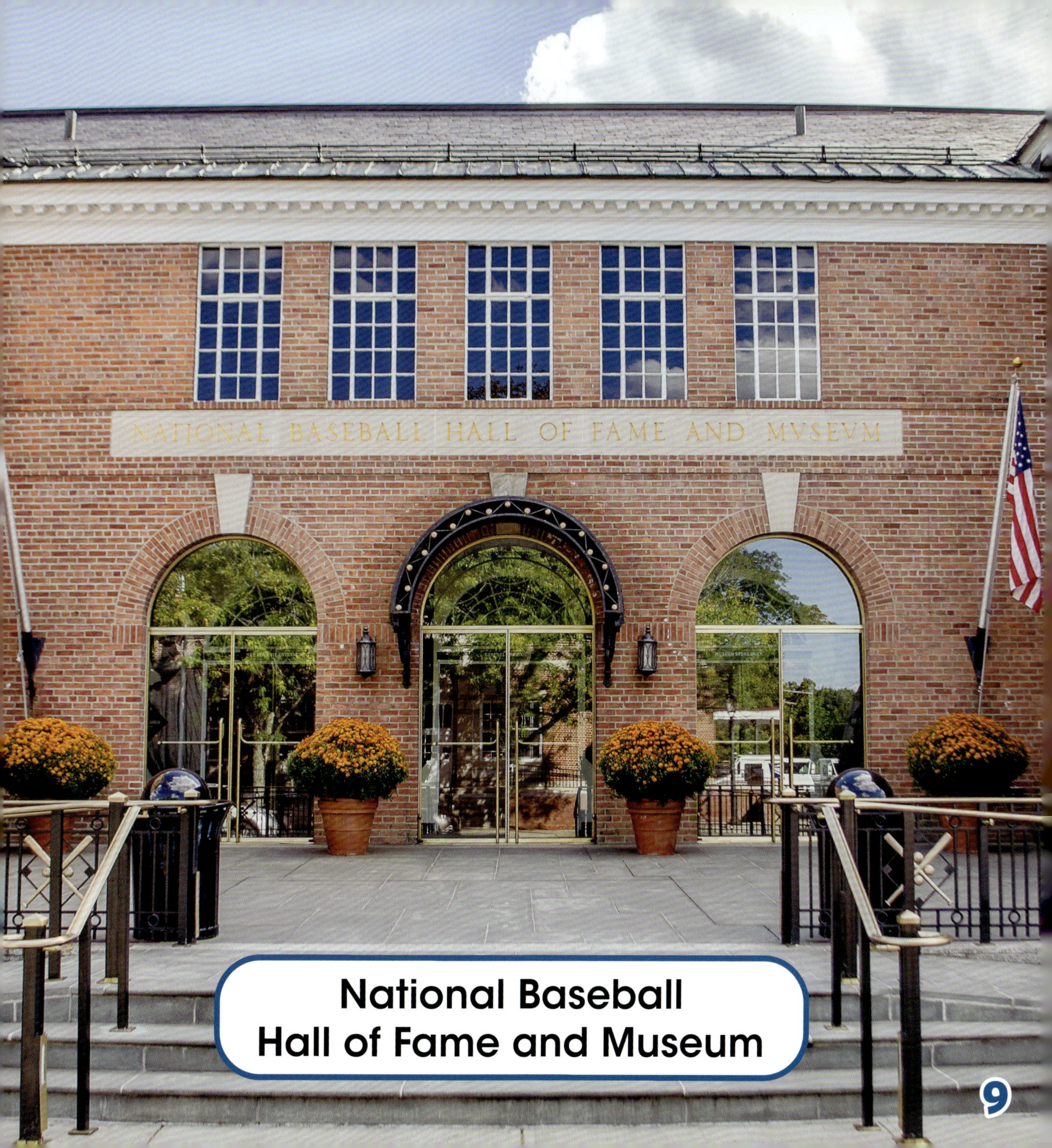

National Baseball
Hall of Fame and Museum

Clemente's First Team

Clemente **improved** how he played baseball by watching Irvin. He copied how Irvin threw and hit the baseball. At only 17, Clemente played well enough to be signed to a professional baseball team. He joined the Santurce Crabbers in Puerto Rico.

Leaving Puerto Rico

But Clemente didn't stop there! The next year, Clemente joined the Brooklyn Dodgers. He was given $10,000 for signing. Instead of playing for the Dodgers though, he played for the Montreal Royals in Canada. The Dodgers lost Clemente in 1954.

IRATES

Playing for the Pirates

Clemente was picked by the Pittsburgh Pirates in 1954. He stayed with the Pirates for the rest of his baseball career. While he was a great player, he still faced a lot of discrimination from baseball fans and other players.

Standing for the People

Clemente spoke up for himself, but also spoke up for all people of color playing baseball. Clemente believed strongly in **charity** work and giving back to the community. Clemente sent food and money to poor communities. He also taught children to play baseball!

Losing Roberto

In 1972, an **earthquake** hit Nicaragua and people needed help. Clemente wanted to make sure the people of Nicaragua got the supplies they needed. On December 31, 1972, Clemente boarded a plane to go to Nicaragua. The plane fell into the ocean and was lost.

K&L GATES
HIGHMARK

Roberto Clemente's Life

Clemente was added to the Baseball Hall of Fame in 1973. He was the first Latin American to be added to the Baseball Hall of Fame. The same year, an award given to players for **sportsmanship** and community service was renamed the Roberto Clemente Award.

Homerun History

August 18, 1934

Roberto Clemente is born in Puerto Rico.

1951

Clemente is signed to his first baseball team, the Santurce Crabbers.

1954

Roberto Clemente joins the Pittsburgh Pirates.

1972

Clemente makes 3,000 hits.

December 31, 1972

Clemente dies in a plane crash.

GLOSSARY

charity: Having to do with giving aid to the poor and suffering.

discrimination: Treating people unfairly based on their race, age, religion, or gender.

earthquake: A shaking of the ground caused by the movement of Earth's crust.

improve: To make something better.

sportsmanship: A way of behaving in sports that includes respecting rules, others, and the outcome of a game.

FOR MORE INFORMATION

BOOKS

Alonso, Nathalie. *Call Me Roberto! Roberto Clemente Goes to Bat for Latinos.* New York, NY: Calkins Creek, 2024.

Hanlon, Luke. *Roberto Clemente: Baseball Legend.* Mendota Heights, MN: Press Box Books, 2024.

WEBSITES

Britannica Kids: Roberto Clemente
kids.britannica.com/kids/article/Roberto-Clemente/390671
Learn more about Roberto Clemente's life and the work that he did.

Wonderopolis: Who Was Roberto Clemente?
wonderopolis.org/wonder/Who-Was-Roberto-Clemente
Learn more about the life of Roberto Clemente.

INDEX